POKÉMON

TOP 10 HANDBOOK

OUR TOP PICKS!

D0562342

BY TRACEY WEST
AND
KATHERINE NOLL

SCHOLASTIC INC.

New York   Toronto   London   Auckland   Sydney
Mexico City   New Delhi   Hong Kong   Buenos Aires

No part of this work may be reproduced in whole or in part, stored in a retrieval system, or transmitted in any form or by any means, electronic, mechanical, photocopying, recording, or otherwise, without written permission of the publisher. For information regarding permission, write to Scholastic Inc., Attention: Permissions Department, 557 Broadway, New York, NY 10012.

ISBN-13: 978-0-545-00161-8
ISBN-10: 0-545-00161-7

© 2006 Pokémon. © 1995-2006 Nintendo/Creatures Inc./ GAME FREAK inc.™ and ® are trademarks of Nintendo. All rights reserved.

Published by Scholastic Inc.

SCHOLASTIC and associated logos are trademarks and/or registered trademarks of Scholastic Inc.

12 11 10 9 8 7 6 5 4   7 8 9 10 11/0

Book Design by Kay Petronio

Printed in the U.S.A.   23

This edition first printing, January 2007

CONTENTS

TEN AWESOME YEARS

Ten years is a long time. It's a whole decade. It's halfway to 20 and one tenth of 100. Ten is a pretty big number.

When most people turn 10, they eat some cake or have a party, right? So what happens when Pokémon turns 10?

Well, Munchlax will probably eat some cake. But Munchlax does that every day. Not so exciting.

No, to celebrate 10 years of Pokémon, you need to do something big. Something huge. Something like a . . .

Book of Pokémon Top 10 Lists!

That's right. In this book, you'll find lots and lots of lists about all things Pokémon. The hottest Fire-type Pokémon. The most sizzling Electric-type Pokémon. The smartest Pokémon experts. The baddest battles. And that's just the beginning.

We've examined every aspect of the Pokémon world to calculate which Pokémon, people, moments, and other things belong on the lists. We've scratched our heads, argued, and worked night and day to get these lists together.

Of course, if you are a real Pokémon fan, a true Pokémaniac, you will probably disagree with everything we have to say.

"No way should that Pokémon be number one!"

"I can't believe it! They left my favorite Pokémon off the list!"

But it's just an opinion. If your opinion is different, go to page 79 of this book. There you can make a list of your own personal best Pokémon of all time.

But before you head to page 79, check out the lists. You may learn something new. You may even agree. And if you don't, you can spend the next 10 years arguing about it!

SECTION 1
POKÉMON TYPES

With nearly 400 known Pokémon in the world, it's not easy to pick just 10 best (although we'll try later on in the book). You probably know that Pokémon can be divided into different types — Fire, Water, Grass, and more. Each type has different strengths and weaknesses. Within each type you can usually find super strong or kind of weak Pokémon.

In this section, we picked 10 types of Pokémon and did a Top 10 list for each one. We also did a bonus list of Top 10 Legendary Pokémon. Here's what we thought about when we came up with our lists:

- To be fair, we kept Legendary Pokémon off all the lists except the Legendary Pokémon list. So you won't find Mewtwo as the number one Psychic-type. We stuck to Pokémon that most Trainers can easily capture and train.
- Some of the Pokémon on the list might be dual-types. Blaziken is a combination Fire-and-Fighting-type Pokémon, but it appears on the Fire-type Pokémon list. A dual-type Pokémon will appear on only one list, not both.
- Super size and strength don't necessarily mean a Pokémon is number one on a list, or even included on a list at all. We looked at a lot of factors when rating Pokémon. A Top 10 Pokémon might be skilled in Contests, or loyal, or versatile in battle, or just super cute! If a Pokémon has been a big help to Ash or his friends, it's probably on the list, too.

Got it? Good! Check out the Pokémon in this section. Can you find your favorites?

TOP 10 FIRE POKÉMON

Can you stand the heat of the hottest Fire-type Pokémon ever? Every good Trainer needs some Fire-type Pokémon in their lineup. If you've got one of these Top 10 scorchers, you'll torch your opponent!

10. CHARMANDER

This is one of the first Pokémon Ash ever caught — and one of the most troublesome! This little Pokemon tested Ash again and again, and helped make Ash the Trainer he is today. Starting out, many Trainers choose a Charmander so they can win battles with its fiery attacks.

9. MAGMAR

We're having a heat wave — any time Magmar is around, that is. The temperature will rise as this Pokémon blows out intensely hot flames from all over its body.

8. MAGCARGO

A volcano in a snail shell — that's Magcargo! This Lava Pokémon is slow and small, but don't let that fool you. Its body is as hot as lava, and flames burst from its shell.

7. RAPIDASH

This fast Pokémon reaches speeds of up to 150 miles per hour while its fiery mane blazes with incredible heat and flames.

6. VULPIX

Vulpix is cute and cuddly, but don't let its looks fool you! This Pokémon is too hot to handle, so give it a hug only if it knows and trusts you. Brock owned a Vulpix once and he knows just how special these Pokémon are.

5. NINETALES

Here's a recipe for a Ninetales: Take one Vulpix, mix with a Fire Stone, and voíla! You've got one powerful Fire-type Pokémon. Fast and fiery, Ninetales is said to live for a thousand years.

4. TORKOAL

One of Ash's favorites, this turtlelike Pokémon just had to be on the Top 10 list. Use its Overheat attack in battle and your opponents won't know what hit them!

3. TYPHLOSION

Everyone knows Ash's Cyndaquil — but who could imagine that one day the cute little Pokémon could evolve into Quilava and then the big and bad Typhlosion? This giant Fire-type Pokémon can cause huge explosions by rubbing the fur on its back together.

2. BLAZIKEN

Blaziken is a combination of Fire-and-Fighting-types, making it one of the strongest Pokémon around. It delivers blazing punches that leave its opponents pleading for mercy. A Blaziken is one of only a few Pokémon to stand up to Ash's Charizard.

1. CHARIZARD

Who else could be the number one Fire-type Pokémon but Charizard? Since Ash found the tiny Charmander, this Fire-type Pokémon has won our hearts and had us cheering for more. It may have been stubborn and difficult at times, but Charizard was always there for Ash and helped him when things got tough. Charizard has faced off against Legendary Pokémon such as Entei and Articuno. Mighty and powerful, Charizard is a must-have for any Trainers who want to leave their foes feeling the burn.

OUR TOP PICKS!
TOP 10 GRASS POKÉMON

Some people think that Grass Pokémon are better off in a garden than a battle arena. Those people should think again! Don't forget — even beautiful roses have thorns.

10. CACNEA

James's Cacnea has been a thorn in Ash's side more than once! This desert dweller attracts prey with the aroma from the flower on its head. Then it shoots it with sharp thorns! Sure, James has been stuck by Cacnea more than once, but with the right Trainer, this sharp shooter can be a great team member.

9. TROPIUS

There aren't too many Pokémon that you can snack on when you get hungry. Tropius is one of them. This Grass-and-Flying-type Pokémon grows delicious fruit around its neck. Children especially love to eat the fruit. It's this amazing quality that puts Tropius on the list.

8. BAYLEEF

Those leaves around Bayleef's neck are really special. They emit a spicy scent that can heal you or make you feel peppy. The smell can also make you want to fight! This energy helps make any battle with a Bayleef special. Ash's Bayleef has some special energy of its own. His playful Pokémon doesn't know its own strength.

7. VILEPLUME

This Grass-and-Poison-type Pokémon has some of the biggest petals in the world. Those petals are filled with poisonous pollen. When an opponent gets close, *bam!* It gets a face full of poison. Now, that's vile!

6. BRELOOM

This Grass-and-Fighting-type Pokémon proves that Grass-types aren't all flowery and sweet. The seeds on its tail release toxic spores that can paralyze its opponent. Then *wham!* Breloom lets loose with a series of quick punches. It's a set of moves that can defeat a wide variety of opponents.

5. VENUSAUR

This Grass-and-Poison-type Pokémon uses the power of the sun when it attacks! The flower on its back captures the sun's rays. It uses that power to unleash a massive Solarbeam attack. Sunscreen won't do much good against this powerhouse.

4. GROVYLE

Ash's Treecko evolved into Grovyle at a key moment—just in time to battle an Exploud. Just like Treecko, Grovyle gives its all in every situation. When Ash battled Norman at Petalburg Gym, Grovyle pounded a fierce Slaking to win the match.

3. TREECKO

When things get hectic, you can always count on Treecko. This cool customer is also a great climber, able to scale vertical walls with the hooks on the bottom of its feet. Ash could always depend on his Treecko. No matter how tough things got, Treecko never gave up!

2. CHIKORITA

Ash's Chikorita was one of his most loyal Pokémon ever. Who can forget when Chikorita evolved into Bayleef just so it could save Ash? Any Trainer would be proud to have this Grass Pokémon on his team.

1. BULBASAUR

Sure, it looks like a cute dinosaur of some kind, but never underestimate this tough little Pokémon. Ash could always rely on his Bulbasaur whenever he needed an edge in battle. And don't forget that May's Bulbasaur defended her from a group of angry Grass-type Pokémon when they first met. You can be sure that Bulbasaur will always have your back!

TOP 10 WATER POKÉMON

You'll make a splash in any battle if you've got a Water-type Pokémon by your side. Feared by Fire-type Pokémon everywhere, these Pokémon can turn any battle into a downpour. Grab an umbrella and get ready to meet the 10 best Water Pokémon ever!

10. STARYU

Misty's Staryu helped her through many battles. Staryu has some interesting features. The center of its body beats like a human heart and glows bright red. And if any of its arms gets damaged, a new one will grow back!

9. STARMIE

One of Misty's most trusted Pokémon, Starmie may be small and not very powerful, but it still has a lot to offer. Loyal and determined, Starmie helped Misty out in many battles.

8. CORSOLA

Misty was so happy when she caught this lovely Pokémon. It continuously sheds its shell-like branches. People use the discarded branches to make beautiful jewelry. You can use it in battle and to make a fashion statement at the same time!

7. MARILL

You just have to smile when this adorable Water-type Pokémon is around. Ash's friend, Tracey Sketchit, was always happy to have his Marill by his side.

6. MILOTIC

Let the good times roll! This beautiful Pokémon has a peaceful effect on anyone who is around it. It can change feelings of anger into calm. Relax and chill out with one of the best Water Pokémon ever!

5. FERALIGATR

Fierce and brutal, Feraligatr's bite is definitely worse than its bark! If this Water-type Pokémon clamps down on you with its powerful jaws, nothing will pry you free.

4. GYARADOS

This larger-than-life Pokémon goes on a rampage any time it appears. Misty was able to overcome her childhood fear of Gyarados to own and train one. Even James got into the Gyarados act when his Magikarp evolved. But he didn't get to keep it for long. Maybe you'll have better luck with this fierce Water Pokémon!

3. TOTODILE

This happy and energetic Pokémon has been making us smile ever since Ash first caught it. Totodile is a reminder that not only big things come in small packages, but powerful ones, too! Its super-strong jaws chomp down hard on its foes.

2. SQUIRTLE

Who can ever forget Ash's first encounter with the Squirtle Squad? Ash found one of his best Pokémon ever in this group of rebels. Now May is enjoying her very own Squirtle, too.

1. BLASTOISE

Blastoise has to be number one because of the strength of its attacks. Pumping out water with enough force to stop even a Charizard, this master blaster will benefit every Trainer who has it in their lineup. Just ask Gary, Ash's rival. His Blastoise helped him win many battles.

TOP 10 NORMAL POKÉMON

OUR TOP PICKS!

There is nothing ordinary about the Normal-type Pokémon on this list. They're just as amazing as other Pokémon that can breathe fire or use psychic powers. Just check out these 10 great Normal-type Pokémon and see what we mean!

10. AZURILL

Misty is finding out just how special this Normal-type Pokémon is. Until it evolves into a Water-type Pokémon, it will bounce for long distances on its rubbery tail. The tail is filled with vitamins to give it energy.

9. SNORLAX

All right, we did say that size would not guarantee a spot on the Top 10, but it's hard to ignore Snorlax! This massive Pokémon weighs 1,014 pounds. Snorlax is best at two things: eating and sleeping. If it's asleep and blocking your path, there's not much you can do — unless you have a Poké Flute.

8. DITTO

This Pokémon has the incredible ability to transform its DNA to take the form of any other Pokémon. Ditto makes an almost perfect copy of the Pokémon, and can even perform its attacks. When it is sleeping, Ditto changes into stone to avoid being attacked.

7. STANTLER

Brock will never forget the time he made friends with a Stantler. At first, Brock thought he was seeing strange things. But it turned out his visions were created by Stantler's amazing antlers. They change the flow of air around them to create a space where reality is distorted. There's nothing normal about that!

6. JIGGLYPUFF

At first glance, there's nothing threatening about this pink Pokémon with big eyes. But just think — how many times has Jigglypuff put Ash and everyone else to sleep by singing its lullaby? And if that's not enough, Jigglypuff likes to draw on the faces of its sleeping victims with Magic Markers. This little Pokémon can cause a lot of trouble!

5. SKITTY

Team Rocket's Meowth would steal a bottle from a baby, but even Meowth has a soft spot for May's adorable Skitty. This kitten-like Pokémon can charm even the toughest customer. May has trained her Skitty to enter and win several Contests.

4. CHANSEY

When you go to a Pokémon Center, you're likely to see a Chansey, or its evolved form, Blissey, helping Nurse Joy. This helpful Pokémon is skilled at taking care of sick Pokémon. It carries around delicious, nutritious eggs.

3. TOGEPI

This adorable little Pokémon is said to bring good luck to people, and its shell is filled with happiness. It definitely brought Misty good luck — and made her happy, too! Misty wasn't sure what to make of the newly hatched Pokémon at first. But Togepi's strange Metronome attack kept Misty and her friends out of danger more than once.

2. EEVEE

Eevee has excellent sight, smell, and hearing. But what makes this the number two Normal-type is its freaky DNA. Its mutated genes can be evolved into five different Pokémon. If you want Jolteon, Vaporeon, Umbreon, Flareon, or Espeon, you've got to start with an Eevee!

1. MEOWTH

Meowth is the heart and soul of Team Rocket, and definitely deserves the number one spot. What other Pokémon would teach itself human speech just to impress a pretty female Meowth? Meowth is funny and clever, and when it's battle time, watch out for its Fury Swipes attack!

TOP 10 ELECTRIC POKÉMON

They're shocking! They're electrifying! They're the 10 best Electric-type Pokémon ever! If you like to zap your opponents, then you must have one of these shockers ready to do battle for you.

10. AMPHAROS

Ampharos is so supercharged, it glows with a powerful bright light that can be seen from space. You can throw out your night-light if you own this amped-up Pokémon!

9. ELECTABUZZ

This Pokémon will be sure to short out your enemies' circuits. Electricity courses over its entire body. Getting near it will make your hair stand on end!

8. PICHU

Awww! Make the adorable Pichu happy and it will evolve into a Pikachu. Who could say no to putting this cutie on our list?

7. PLUSLE

Who wouldn't want Plusle on their side during a battle? Always supportive, this sweet Electric-type Pokémon will cry if its partner loses.

6. MINUN

Both Minun and Plusle are the cheerleaders of the Pokémon world. Who needs fireworks when this delightful little Pokémon sends out showers of sparks to cheer its teammates on?

5. MAGNETON

When three Magnemite get together, they form a powerful Magneton. The magnetic power of this Pokémon is so strong that when several Magneton get together, they can shut down entire cities!

4. JOLTEON

Time to dodge a few lightning bolts! Jolteon tosses wicked ones at its foes. Each bolt throws out 10,000 volts! When you battle with this Pokémon, you are sure to shock everyone.

3. MANECTRIC

Manectric is an awesome Electric-type Pokémon to have at the ready. Super strong, its attacks are very effective against its enemies. Manectric collects electricity from the air, using its mane. Then thunderclouds appear above its head!

2. RAICHU

The final, evolved form of Pichu and Pikachu, Raichu is a powerful jolt of electrical energy packaged into a mouselike body. When its body is charged with a lot of energy, it will glow in the dark!

1. PIKACHU

Of course Pikachu's at the number one spot! What did you expect? We love this little Pokémon so much. Not only is it Ash's best friend, this brave and loyal Electric Pokémon has also become a hero to Pokémon fans all around the world. Thunder on, Pikachu!

We all know that Pokémon are never bad or evil — they're just following their nature, or obeying their Trainer. But there's no doubt that there's something slightly sinister about most Dark-type Pokémon. Some are creepy, some are spooky, and most are hard to beat.

10. HOUNDOUR

Even before they evolve into Houndoom, these Fire-and-Dark-type Pokémon are a force to be reckoned with. They travel in packs, and they look out for each other. Once, a Houndour stole Ash's backpack to help an injured member of its pack. Houndour don't normally trust humans, but they let Ash help, proving they'll do anything to help one of their own.

9. NUZLEAF

Nuzleaf live in forests, and it is said that these Grass-and-Dark-type Pokémon like to scare people passing by. Once, a family of Nuzleaf captured the Pokémon belonging to Ash and his friends. It turned out to be a misunderstanding, but that was still a pretty bold move.

8. CACTURNE

Cacturne is like a walking nightmare. This Grass-and-Dark-type Pokémon looks like a scarecrow during the day, but at night, it comes to life. It lays in wait for weary travelers. When they grow tired, Cacturne attacks.

7. SHARPEDO

This combination Water-and-Dark-type is widely feared by sailors. It swims at 75 miles per hour. Its teeth can tear through iron, and Sharpedo will destroy anything that comes into its territory. For that reason it's known as the Bully of the Sea.

6. SNEASEL

This Dark-and-Ice-type Pokémon is most feared for its sharp claws. They stay hidden in its paws until it is time to attack. Then they lash out.

5. MURKROW

It's easy to spot a Murkrow perched on a wire or in a tree, but you may not want to. People say that this Dark-and-Flying-type Pokémon brings bad luck if it is seen at night.

4. UMBREON

Known as the Moonlight Pokémon, Umbreon waits in the darkness and leaps out at its prey. It can spray poisonous sweat from its pores. The rings around its body glow when it is about to attack, or under a full moon.

3. ABSOL

Absol is called the Disaster Pokémon because it appears just before a natural disaster such as a flood or earthquake, happens. For a long time, people thought Absol was causing the disasters, and thought the Pokémon to be bad luck. But now researchers believe that it wants to warn humans of the coming danger.

2. MIGHTYENA

If you want this Bite Pokémon on your team, you've got to have superior skills as a Trainer. Otherwise, Mightyena won't obey you. Then you may find yourself on the wrong end of its sharp teeth!

1. HOUNDOOM

A combination of Dark-and-Fire-types, Houndoom is a snarling, terrifying opponent. Be careful of the flames it shoots from its mouth! Houndoom travel in packs. To choose a leader, they fight among themselves.

TOP 10 ROCK POKÉMON

It's time to rock out — the ten best Rock-type Pokémon are here. Trying to break down the defenses of one of them is like trying to smash through a brick wall with a Caterpie!

10. SUDOWOODO

It's a Rock Pokémon that pretends to be a tree! Sudowoodo blends in well in the forest or a wooded park. But its body is really made up of a rocklike substance. In your travels, you might encounter a Sudowoodo who will block your way.

Here's a tip: This Rock-type Pokémon doesn't like water.

9. CRADILY

This Pokémon doesn't only look strange — it is truly unique. A combination Rock-and-Grass-type, Cradily lives in the ocean. Look out for its tentacles — it grabs on to its prey and doesn't let go!

8. ARMALDO

The small Anorith evolves into the powerful Armaldo. With its enormous claws, hard shell, and sturdy body, this Rock-and-Bug-type Pokémon is a tough nut to crack.

7. AERODACTYL

This ferocious prehistoric Pokémon once tried to eat Ash for dinner. Luckily, Charmeleon evolved into Charizard and saved the day. Otherwise, we would have said a sad good-bye to Ash Ketchum! Try and see if you can tame this mighty Rock-and-Flying-type Pokémon. (Hint: You might want to keep a Charizard around in case Aerodactyl gets hungry!)

6. RHYDON

From its super-sharp horn to its thick-as-rock skin, Rhydon is one formidable foe. It crushes the competition with its grinding strength.

5. AGGRON

If you want to rock the Pokémon world, Aggron is the one for you. This Steel-and-Rock-type is a lot like Tyranitar. It's difficult to penetrate its defenses. And Aggron is very protective of its mountain habitat. It will pummel anything that tries to crash its turf.

4. RELICANTH

Ash first spotted this ancient Pokémon in a secret underground chamber. This Water-and-Rock-type is a living link to the past. Ash encountered Relicanth again, when he and his friends were trapped in an under-water cave after searching for a sunken ship. A school of Relicanth led them to safety!

3. GEODUDE

Every good Rock-type Trainer needs this Pokémon. Brock owned a Geodude and always relied on it in battle. This sturdy Pokémon can evolve into the even stronger Graveler and finally into the super-tough Golem.

2. TYRANITAR

This Rock-and-Dark-type Pokémon might just be one of the most powerful Pokémon around. Tyranitar's body can't be harmed by any attacks. And its own attacks are earth-shaking — literally. The ground moves when this Pokémon is in action.

1. ONIX

Brock's Onix saved Brock and his friends on more than one occasion. This tremendously strong Rock Pokémon can tunnel through the ground at speeds of over 50 mph. Brock is very close to his Onix, his first Pokémon ever. Brock's dad gave it to him on his tenth birthday.

TOP 10 FLYING POKÉMON

Flying-type Pokémon are great because they have the advantage of attacking from the air, above their opponent. Most Flying Pokémon are dual-types, so we picked Pokémon for this list that are best known for their aerial abilities.

10. SPEAROW

The loud cry of this Pokémon can be heard for miles. It is very protective of its territory. When Spearow flock together, they can mean big trouble. When Ash first got his Pikachu, a flock of these Flying-types nearly destroyed the poor little Pokémon!

9. ZUBAT

Brock's Zubat came in handy many times during his journeys with Ash and Misty. If a Pokémon got lost, or was stolen by Team Rocket, Zubat could fly overhead and use Supersonic to locate the missing Pokémon.

8. TOGETIC

Okay, so this Happiness Pokémon is not known for being great at flight. Its short wings don't do much, and Togetic can't fly without using them! What's special about this Normal-and-Flying-type is that it makes people happy just by being around. And who can't use a little extra happiness in life?

7. NOCTOWL

When traveling through the Johto region, Ash relied on this Normal-and-Flying-type Pokémon a lot. Noctowl was great at popping Team Rocket's balloon! Noctowl can see in the dark, and can rotate its head 180 degrees, so it always knows what's coming. Its soft wings make no sound in flight, which means it can sneak up on its prey without being detected.

6. SWELLOW

Ash used this graceful Pokémon in some of his Gym battles in the Hoenn region. Maybe that's because Swellow can defend itself against many types of attacks, including Electric ones. Another feature of this Normal-and-Flying-type are its claws. Once it captures prey in its strong talons, there's no escape!

5. FEAROW

These striking Pokémon have huge and magnificent wings. They never need to rest when they're flying. A Fearow will use its long, thin beak to attack or to snatch prey from the ground or in water.

4. ALTARIA

Most Dragon-and-Flying-types have amazing abilities, and Altaria is no exception. When it flies through the clouds, it looks like it's dancing gracefully. Don't let Altaria's beauty fool you. Ash has battled an Altaria twice — and he beat it only one of those times.

3. SKARMORY

The combination of Steel-and-Flying-types makes this Pokémon unique. Its sturdy wings are hollow and light, allowing Skarmory to fly at speeds of up to 190 miles per hour. Its feathers are so sharp, they were once used as swords!

2. PIDGEOTTO

This might be a fairly common Pokémon, but it's a useful one to have on your team. Pidgeotto has excellent vision and can spot prey from great heights. It fiercely pecks intruders that get into its territory. Just ask Ash what a Pidgeotto can do — it was one of Ash's first Pokémon.

1. DRAGONITE

As you can guess from its name, this rare Pokémon is also a Dragon-type. Ash first faced a Dragonite in battle against Drake of the Orange Islands. Dragonite took down his Charizard! Pikachu stepped in to beat Dragonite, but it was a tough battle. Charizard had a chance to battle Dragonite again when Ash traveled to Blackthorn City. This time, Charizard won!

TOP 10 BUG POKÉMON

Put away the insect repellent. Drop that flyswatter! The best Bug-type Pokémon of all time will not drive you buggy — but they just might sting and pester your opponents until they beg for mercy.

10. WURMPLE

Wurmple is an interesting Pokémon that can evolve into two different kinds of Bug Pokémon. At certain times during the day, it will become a Silcoon. But other times, you'd become the owner of a Cascoon. May and Jessie once got their Wurmple mixed up — they didn't know whose was whose!

9. PINECO

When Brock first saw his Pineco, it exploded right in his face! That didn't stop Brock from capturing and training this Bug-type. Pineco ended up helping out whenever Brock needed an extra boost in battle.

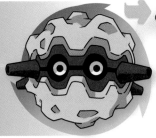

8. FORRETRESS

Brock's pal Forretress evolved from Pineco just in time to save everyone from one of Team Rocket's harebrained schemes. Its steel-hard shell gives Forretress a lot of protection.

7. DUSTOX

Jessie's Wurmple evolved into a Cascoon, which became a Dustox. Jessie wept tears of joy when she saw it for the first time. Dustox is a Bug-and-Poison-type, and we know how Jessie likes Poison Pokémon! Jessie enters Dustox in Contests, and usually cheats. If only she knew how to train this unique Pokémon, she wouldn't have to!

6. BEAUTIFLY

Beautifly is so, well — beautiful! It starts out as a Wurmple. May was delighted when her Wurmple evolved into a Silcoon — and soon into Beautifly! May has been entering this talented Pokémon in Contests ever since.

5. NINJASK

One of the hardest Pokémon to train, this Bug-and-Flying-type Pokémon is the true test of how good a Trainer you really are. Ninjask moves so fast that for years many people believed it was invisible!

4. SCYTHER

This Pokémon has ninja-like ability and speed. Its arms are razor-sharp scythes. Tracey Sketchit added a Scyther to his team, and the Pokémon proved to be a fierce competitor, picking fights with Ash's Charizard.

3. HERACROSS

After Ash helped a Heracross save its forest from a group of destructive Pinsir, he added the sweet yet strong Pokémon to his collection and was glad he did! This physically powerful Bug-and-Fighting-type Pokémon can lift and throw an object that is 100 times its own weight.

2. BEEDRILL

No Pokémon is as busy as a Beedrill when it comes to chasing down its enemies. A furious swarm of Beedrill once had Ash and his friends on the run. Eventually, Ash caught a Beedrill of his own, but he gave it away to another Trainer.

1. BUTTERFREE

The very first Pokémon Ash ever caught was a Caterpie. It evolved into Metapod and then into the lovely but-terfly-like Pokémon Butterfree! One flap of its wings sends a shower of poisonous powder down on its enemies.
Ash always puts his Pokémon first, and Butterfree was no exception. He said good-bye to the first Pokémon he caught so it could go and start a family.

TOP 10 PSYCHIC POKÉMON

If you can read our minds, then you know that we think Psychic-type Pokémon are really cool! Most types find their Psychic attacks difficult to overcome. Their mysterious moves are always exciting. Let's take a look to see which of them made the Top 10.

10. CHIMECHO

This Pokémon may look like a cute wind chime, but you don't want to be near it if it gets angry. Its ultrasonic screams are so powerful, they can send foes flying! But even James from Team Rocket appreciates its sweet and soothing qualities — he won't let it battle.

9. WOBBUFFET

Jessie's Wobbuffet always seems to be popping up when she doesn't want it to. This strange Pokémon might look a little weird, but it has strength and stamina. If two Wobbuffet meet, they may face off to see which will last the longest. They'll go on and on without eating or sleeping until one of them falls!

8. GIRAFARIG

What makes this Normal-and-Psychic-type special is that it has two brains! Its tail has a tiny brain of its own. If you get too close, watch out! Girafarig's tail will bite.

7. KIRLIA

The horns on its head magnify the power created by Kirlia's highly developed brain. The air around Kirlia can become distorted, creating mirages. Maybe that's why the illusionist Butler used a Kirlia in the film *Pokémon: Jirachi Wishmaker*.

6. MEDICHAM

The fact that Medicham is a Psychic-and-Fighting-type gives it an edge over other Psychic Pokémon. Its Fighting moves can do damage to Pokémon immune to Psychic-type attacks. Medicham still has awesome psychic powers. It can meditate for a whole month without eating, to increase its energy and heighten its sixth sense.

5. SLOWKING

How does the dopey Slowpoke evolve into the super-smart Slowking? Some say that the Shellder on its head injects Slowking with a kind of poison that gives its brainpower a boost. In the Orange Islands, Ash met a Slowking capable of real human speech, an extremely rare skill for a Pokémon.

4. SOLROCK

Did this Rock-and-Psychic-type fall from space? That's what some people think. Solrock has the power of the sun and can read the emotions of others. In battle, it releases an intensely bright light.

3. LUNATONE

Like Solrock, researchers think this Pokémon fell from space. Lunatone becomes active during a full moon. Anyone who looks into its red eyes will become transfixed with fear.

2. ESPEON

Espeon can predict its enemy's actions using the fine hairs on its body, which sense the movement of air currents around it. It has developed powers to protect its Trainer from harm, which makes it one of the most loyal Pokémon around. Villains Annie and Oakley used an Espeon and an Ariados to capture Legendary Pokémon Latias and Latios.

1. ALAKAZAM

Maybe the most intelligent Pokémon around, Alakazam's brain is like a super-computer. It has an IQ of 5,000! Alakazam can memorize anything it wants to, and it never forgets what it learns. Just imagine facing this genius in battle!

OUR TOP PICKS!

TOP 10 LEGENDARY POKÉMON

Mysterious. Powerful. Rare. Their talents are many. Their powers are unsurpassed. Meet the Top 10 Legendary Pokémon of all time. Try to learn their secrets — if you dare.

10. CELEBI

Guardian of the forest, Celebi appears in beautiful wooded areas. This Grass-and-Psychic-type Pokémon can travel across time. Just ask Ash. He had to help a boy named Sammy who was pulled 40 years into the future by Celebi!

9. SUICUNE

Ash and his friends have been lucky enough to spot this rare Water-type Pokémon. Suicune has the unusual but useful power to purify polluted water.

8. ENTEI

Fiery and fierce, Entei can run at super speed and shoots out massive bursts of flames. Once, Ash's mother was kidnapped by an Entei that was trying to fulfill the wishes of a girl named Molly. Ash and Charizard battled Entei, but couldn't beat this Legendary beast. Only after Molly changed her mind was Ash's mother freed.

7. JIRACHI

This Pokémon is believed to make wishes come true! This little wish maker wakes up only once every thousand years. Max became best friends with Jirachi and was very sad when it had to leave.

6. LUGIA

Big and strong, Lugia lives under the ocean. The guardian of the sea, it rarely comes out. Lugia emerged once to help put a stop to the battling of Articuno, Zapdos, and Moltres, saving the world. Ash once helped reunite a kidnapped baby Lugia with its parent!

5. MEWTWO

The complex Mewtwo was created in a lab, using Mew's DNA. A very smart and power-ful Psychic-type Pokémon, Mewtwo will do whatever it thinks is right — regardless of who gets hurt along the way.

4. KYOGRE

The massive Water-type Pokémon Kyogre controls rain clouds and has saved many people during times of drought. When Groudon and Kyogre cross paths, watch out! Their battles disturb the weather and have catastrophic consequences for people everywhere.

3. GROUDON

The giant Ground-type Pokémon Groudon can control the land by raising continents. It has been seen as a savior to people suffering from floods. Groudon can make water evaporate. But its ancient grudge against Kyogre causes huge problems for the entire world.

2. RAYQUAZA

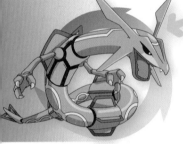

If you are strong enough to catch this Legendary Pokémon, you must do so immediately. Rayquaza's strength and speed are unmatched by any other Pokémon. It lives high in the sky and comes down to Earth only when its territory is in jeopardy — like when Groudon and Kyogre battle, or when Deoxys appeared. Rayquaza can stop the chaos and save the day!

1. MEW

Mew contains the DNA of all Pokémon everywhere. It is said to be the ancestor of all Pokémon. Without Mew, no other Pokémon would exist. This is why Mew has earned the top spot in the Legendary list.

SECTION 2 POKÉMON PEOPLE

Yes, we know that Pokémon is all about, well — Pokémon! But the world of Pokémon wouldn't be the same without the human characters that make it tick.

First, you've got Pokémon Trainers, those dedicated boys and girls, men and women, who dedicate their lives to taking care of Pokémon. Then there are Gym Leaders, experienced Trainers who give up-and-comers a chance to earn badges and improve their skills. And of course there are Pokémon experts; researchers who are walking encyclopedias of information about Pokémon.

Of course, not all Pokémon characters are hardworking or helpful. There are plenty of bad guys (and girls) out there who try to steal Pokémon or use them for their own evil purposes. We'll take a look at those characters, too.

Do you think you know who has earned a place on these lists? You may be in for some surprises. But you won't know unless you turn the page!

TOP 10 TRAINERS

At the age of 10, every kid is old enough to get a license to train Pokémon. At the start of their journey, they're allowed to choose a Fire-, Grass-, or Water-type Pokémon. Some Trainers go on to win battles, badges, and championships. Others become Pokémon experts. And some can't take the heat and give up. You won't find any of *those* Trainers on this Top 10 list!

10. NOLAND

Noland is one of the "Brains" of the Battle Frontier in the Kanto region. Trainers who enter the Frontier get an opportunity to have some amazing battles. Noland is notable because he has befriended a Legendary Pokémon, Articuno, and can battle with it. His Articuno faced off against Ash's Charizard in a memorable battle.

9. RICHIE

When Ash entered the Pokémon Indigo League Tournament, he met Richie. This young Trainer was like Ash in a lot of ways. He went on to beat Ash in the tournament, although some would blame that loss on Ash's Charizard. Richie has kept up his training, and turned up in time to protect Moltres from Butch and Cassidy.

8. DRAKE

Don't confuse this Drake with the one from the Orange Islands. The Drake we're talking about is one of the Elite Four of the Hoenn region. Drake specializes in Dragon-types and when he faced Ash, he won the battle using his Altaria. Even though he won, he took the time to give Ash some great tips about not being overly confident in battle.

7. LANCE

Lance is a Trainer with a mission—to go undercover and stop evildoers from harming Pokémon. He once helped Ash defeat Team Rocket and catch the red Gyarados they had created as part of their sinister experiments. He was also instrumental in stopping a massive battle between Groudon and Kyogre.

6. AGATHA

When Professor Oak was a young Trainer, Agatha was his rival. Professor Oak went on to become one of the world's greatest Pokémon experts. Agatha concentrated on battling with her Ghost-type Pokémon to become a member of the Elite Four in the Kanto region. It's not easy to beat this experienced Trainer!

5. GARY OAK

When Ash first met his rival, Gary was overconfident and rude. But he did have the skills to back it up. Gary often beat Ash in battle, and went on to win many Gym badges. He even defeated villains Butch and Cassidy in a battle. Over time, Gary became a little bit nicer. He retired from competition to become a researcher like his grandfather, Professor Oak.

4. MAY

One of the reasons May is a great Trainer is because she started out being a little afraid of her Pokémon, but overcame her fears. She puts a lot of love and energy into her training, and she really found her strength when she decided to enter her Pokémon in Pokémon Contests instead of battling with them. She's taught her Skitty, Beautifly, Combusken, and Bulbasaur some pretty amazing skills!

3. BROCK

When your Pokémon are hungry, when you need someone to back you up in battle, when you need a solution to a problem, Brock is always there to help! This well-rounded Trainer is well on his way to being an expert in Pokémon breeding. He knows how to take care of Pokémon as well as use their strengths in battle. That makes Brock one of the best Trainers around.

2. MISTY

She's always up for an adventure. She never backs down from a challenge. She's also a great example of what can happen when a Trainer decides to specialize in one type of Pokémon. Misty loves her Water-type Pokémon, and knows exactly how to use them to win.

1. ASH KETCHUM

There's absolutely no question that Ash is the number one Pokémon Trainer of all time. We could list all of the battles and badges that he's won, but that's just a small part of it. Nobody — and we mean nobody — is more dedicated to Pokémon than Ash. He will go anywhere and battle anyone to increase his skills as a Trainer. Ash will also take time to help other Trainers. And that's not all. He's also saved the world a few times! If that doesn't earn him the number one spot, we don't know what does.

TOP 10 BAD GUYS

Boo! Hiss! The bad guys are here! After 10 years of Pokémon, we've got to admit there are a few who have grown on us. (Such as the always bumbling Team Rocket.) But for the most part, if you spot one of these criminals, guard your Pokémon and make a fast exit!

10. LAWRENCE III

This guy doesn't like or respect Pokémon — he just wants to collect them because he's greedy. In *Pokémon the Movie 2000*, his attempt to capture the Legendary birds Zapdos, Moltres, and Articuno nearly destroyed the world!

9. IRON MASKED MARAUDER

What makes this villain a well-known member of Team Rocket? He likes to capture innocent Pokémon in a Dark Ball, which increases their power and makes them act evil. Then he uses them for his own sinister purposes. This creep once used a Dark Ball on a poor little Celebi!

8. BUTCH

Butch is Cassidy's partner in crime. He has a rivalry with James. Butch, along with Cassidy, gets arrested a lot more than Jessie and James. But Giovanni always comes and bails out his faves!

7. CASSIDY

Along with her partner Butch, Cassidy is a part of Team Rocket that is actually successful. Cassidy does not like Jessie and is constantly putting her down. Both Cassidy and Butch are Giovanni's favorites because they actually steal Pokémon and deliver them to the boss. Cassidy's favorite trick is to pretend to be a Pokémon breeder and get Trainers to leave their Pokémon with her. But when they come back to pick up their Pokémon, it's too late! Cassidy and Butch have already sent them to Giovanni.

6. ARCHIE

The wicked opposite of Team Magma, Archie's Team Aqua wants to capture Kyogre to flood the lands and make more room for Water-type Pokémon. Team Magma and Team Aqua are always fighting. Let's hope neither of them accomplishes their evil schemes.

5. MAXIE

Leader of the evil Team Magma, Maxie and his crew are trying to capture the mighty Groudon so that the oceans dry up. Team Magma doesn't like Water Pokémon. They want to make room for land-based Pokémon.

4. MEOWTH

This Pokémon is the brains behind Jessie and James. (And that's not saying much.) This talking Pokémon always daydreams about surprising Giovanni with a rare stolen Pokémon. Meowth's dreams never come true because the twerps are always ruining its plans!

3. JAMES

James lets Jessie boss him around a lot. We know there is a heart of gold inside this Pokémon thief. Maybe Jessie and James will give up their harebrained schemes and go into the field in which their talents really lie — fashion design! Their disguises are awesome, and they always manage to fool Ash and his friends.

2. JESSIE

She is definitely the tough one in Team Rocket. But we've seen her cry and even do the right thing! Maybe one day Jessie can give up her bad-girl ways and come over to the good side.

1. GIOVANNI

Much more than your ordinary Gym Leader, Giovanni wants to collect all of the most valuable Pokémon and rule the world! Giovanni was behind the creation of Mewtwo. He is constantly training new villains to do his dirty work for him and the Team Rocket organization. Without Giovanni, the Pokémon world would be a much safer place.

TOP 10 POKÉMON EXPERTS

They might not be heroes on the battlefield, but without their knowledge most Trainers would be at a loss. These experts spend all their spare time studying Pokémon so that humans and Pokémon can have the best relationship possible. For that, we salute them!

10. MAX

Sure, May's younger brother is just a kid — not even old enough to get his Pokémon license. But bookworm Max has read just about everything written about Pokémon, and he knows a lot. He'll probably make a great professor someday.

9. KURT

He might be a little bit cranky, but there's nobody else who knows how to make Poké Balls from apricorns like Kurt does. He takes these odd fruits of different colors and transforms them into different kinds of Poké Balls.

8. PROFESSOR SERENA

Every official Pokémon battle needs a judge. To be a battle judge, you need to be an expert on battle rules and Pokémon moves. So who trains the judges? That would be Professor Serena, of the Pokémon Battle Judge Training Institute. If you think you've got what it takes to be a judge, look her up on Bomba Island in the Hoenn region.

7. LIZA

We're not talking about the Gym Leader named Liza, but the amazing woman who trains Charizard in the Charicific Valley. Charizard are huge and powerful, and can be incredibly stubborn. It takes smarts and strength to tame these Pokémon, and Liza has what it takes.

6. PROFESSOR ELM

A former student of Professor Oak, Professor Elm went on to become an expert who lives in the Johto region. Like Oak, he can be a little bit absentminded, but nobody knows more about Pokémon Evolution and breeding than Professor Elm.

5. TRACEY SKETCHIT

Ash met this Trainer on his journeys in the Orange Islands. Tracey's goal is to become a Pokémon watcher. At a glance, he can tell if your Pokémon's color is off or if it needs more exercise. He currently works as Professor Oak's assistant.

4. PROFESSOR IVY

You'll find this professor in a large lab on Valencia Island. She is best known for discovering the GS Ball — and for breaking Brock's heart (although he won't talk about it). When Moltres, Zapdos, and Articuno were threatening the world, Professor Ivy was one of two experts called on to investigate the case.

3. PROFESSOR BIRCH

Most professors spend their days cooped up in a lab, but not Professor Birch. He prefers to be out in the field, studying Pokémon in the wild. He lives in the Hoenn region and is in charge of giving Trainers there their starter Pokémon.

2. NURSE JOY

Your Pokémon fainted in battle! It's sick and you don't know why! What do you do? Head to the nearest Pokémon Center — and find Nurse Joy. No matter which Nurse Joy you meet, you'll find someone who knows exactly what to do to heal your Pokémon. The world would be very sad without Nurse Joy!

1. PROFESSOR OAK

Whenever Ash has a question about his Pokémon, he turns to Professor Oak. Once a competitive Trainer, Professor Oak now devotes his time to studying Pokémon and helping young Trainers work better with their Pokémon. This brilliant guy is also the inventor of the Pokédex.

TOP 10 GYM LEADERS

You've probably battled some of these Gym Leaders — or maybe you watched Ash take them on. Either way, you know that defeating Gym Leaders is the key to earning badges. Train your Pokémon and then face these Top 10 Gym Leaders in the battle of a lifetime!

10. MORTY

A Ghost-type Pokémon specialist from Ecruteak City, this mysterious Trainer will leave you shaking in your shoes. Morty gets extra points for being able to find lost objects and see things from a distance. He's also an expert on several Legendary Pokémon.

9. LT. SURGE

A bit of a bully, this Electric Trainer is the Vermillion City Gym Leader. His Raichu is super strong — but Pikachu managed to win the day and earn Ash his Thunder Badge.

8. FLANNERY

This fiery Gym Leader has a real love for Fire-type Pokémon. Go to the Lavaridge Town Gym and see if you can beat her Torkoal and two Magcargo!

7. WINONA

A battle in the sky — that's what you get when you challenge Winona at the Fortree City Gym. Perched on platforms high above the ground, you must defend against this flying Trainer's Skarmory, Swellow, Pelipper, and Altaria.

6. NORMAN

May and Max's dad Norman is a Normal-type Pokémon Trainer who is the Gym Leader in Petalburg City. Watch out for his super-strong Slaking. It can pound your Pokémon into the ground.

5. TATE AND LIZA

It's double trouble at the Mossdeep City Gym! Tate and Liza are twins and if you want to earn a Mind Badge, you'll have to beat them both at the same time in a double battle. Tate's Solrock and Liza's Lunatone are both tough, so you'll have to stay sharp to beat these Psychic-type Trainers and their Pokémon!

4. JUAN

The smooth-talking Juan is not only the Sootopolis City Gym Leader — he is also a celebrity! Hundreds of fans come out to watch his battles. If you can beat this Water-type Pokémon specialist, maybe you'll make a few fans of your own!

3. ERIKA

If you are looking to take on a Gym Leader who specializes in Grass-types, Erika is your woman! You can find her at the Celadon City Gym. When she is not making perfume, Erika will battle you with her Tangela, Weepinbell, and Gloom.

2. SABRINA

This creepy psychic Trainer almost ended Ash's journey early. A spoon-bending, mind-twisting opponent, Sabrina can be found at the Saffron City Gym. Battle her — but be prepared!

1. MISTY

Misty number one? We had to give it to the red-haired girl who knows all there is to know about Water-types. She left behind her best friends to return to the Cerulean City Gym and take over as Gym Leader.

SECTION 3 ACTION

There's no other feeling like it. You face off against another Trainer, not knowing what Pokémon they're going to choose. For the next few minutes, you've got to focus your thoughts on the battle. You've got to choose your Pokémon and their moves wisely, or else you'll lose the battle. Time seems to stand still as the action unfolds. . . .

Whether you like to battle your Pokémon or just watch Pokémon battles, you have to admit they're an amazing spectacle. In this section, we'll take a look at the best moves, best places to go, best battles, and more. Check out some of the people, places, and things that have really rocked the Pokémon world!

TOP 10 ATTACKS

If you want to be a master Trainer, you'll need to make sure your Pokémon know these moves. These attacks have made it to the top 10 list because they are sure to leave your foes' Pokémon in a faint — or close enough for you to finish them off!

10. RECOVER

Is your Pokémon in trouble? If so, it's really helpful to know this move. Recover can restore up to half of your Pokémon's energy, giving it the will to battle on.

9. AERIAL ACE

This Flying-type attack never misses. If you need a surefire hit, then go with a Flying Pokémon that knows Aerial Ace.

8. SOLAR BEAM

Sit back and watch as your Grass-type Pokémon takes in sunlight and blasts your opponent with this powerful move.

7. HYPER BEAM

This Normal-type attack can be used against almost any type. It's a tough attack and a good all-purpose move to have in your Pokémon lineup.

6. EARTHQUAKE

Shake up any Pokémon battle with this strong Ground-type attack. It effects all Pokémon on the field, so if you need to have everyone running for cover, this is the attack for you.

5. PSYCHIC

With this powerful attack, you will make your foe's head spin. Good against almost every type, this attack is the reason most Trainers want a Psychic-type Pokémon on their roster.

4. ICE BEAM

Ice Beam is so cool — no, really it's freezing! Are you facing a fierce Dragon Pokémon? Then make sure your Ice Pokémon knows this awesome move. The Dragon-type won't know what hit it.

3. FLAMETHROWER

This Fire-type attack gives Grass-type Pokémon nightmares. Engulfed in flames, a Pokémon who has Flamethrower tossed at it has little hope of recovery.

2. HYDRO PUMP

This is super strong against almost any type, except Grass. This water attack will leave your opponents drenched!

1. THUNDER

Incredibly strong, this is the most powerful Electric-type attack. You'll send your foes flying when you use this jolting move. It's super effective against Water- and Flying-types, so if you want to knock out one of these, make sure you've got a Pokémon who can perform Thunder.

TOP 10 ITEMS

Head on over to the nearest PokéMart or Pokémon Department Store and grab one of these items. They may not all be essential for battling, but you'll find that these items can really come in handy.

10. POKÉFLUTE

Is a massive Snorlax blocking your path? Is it sleeping and you can't budge it? Then do what Ash and Misty did and get your hands on a PokéFlute. The notes of this instrument can wake a sleeping Snorlax.

9. KING'S ROCK

Do you like Misty's Politoed? To get one of your own, you'll need a King's Rock. Use it with a trade to evolve your Poliwhirl into this unusual Water Pokémon. It's also a key ingredient in turning a Slowpoke into a Slowking.

8. MOON STONE

With this rare stone, you can make some of the most interesting Pokémon evolutions happen. Evolve a Skitty into a Delcatty, Clefairy into Clefable, or Jigglypuff into Wigglytuff.

7. DRAGON FANG

This item is so rare that Team Rocket tried to steal one from the Blackthorn Gym. If you have Dragon Pokémon, you can use Dragon Fang to increase the power of their already powerful attacks!

6. WATER STONE

When Brock's Lotad fell in love with a Mawile, it used a Water Stone to evolve into Ludicolo. You can also use a Water Stone to evolve Poliwhirl, Shellder, Staryu, and Eevee.

5. THUNDER STONE

A Thunder Stone is a must-have to evolve certain Electric types. Of course, not all Pokémon want to evolve. Ash's Pikachu had the chance to use a Thunder Stone to evolve into Raichu, but it refused!

4. MAX POTION

When a Pokémon takes a hard hit in battle, you can use a Potion to help get it back on its feet. Max Potion is the ultimate Potion to use, because it has the strongest effect.

3. POKÉBLOCK

These tasty treats can increase the stats of your Pokémon so it can win contests. May is learning how to make PokéBlocks from Poké berries to help her Pokémon improve. So far, her Munchlax is the only one who will eat them.

2. POKÉNAV

This handy device doubles as a communicator and a navigator. May's little brother Max took charge of her PokéNav, and he uses it to help May and the others decide where to go next.

1. POKÉDEX

Where would Ash be without his Pokédex? This mini computer is an electronic encyclopedia containing information about all things Pokémon. It's the most important thing any Trainer can own.

TOP 10 POKÉ BALLS

Gotta catch 'em all, right? Well, you can't catch anything without a Poké Ball. There are all kinds of Poké Balls with all kinds of uses, but we've narrowed them down to the 10 best.

10. DARK BALL

We don't really like Dark Balls, but you can't deny their power. A Pokémon captured by a Dark Ball will turn into a dark, sinister version of itself, with stronger powers.

9. HEAVY BALL

If you want to catch something big, like an Onix or a Snorlax, this ball can make the job easier.

8. SAFARI BALL

You've got to have one if you want to catch wild Pokémon in the Kanto or Hoenn region's Safari Zone.

7. FRIEND BALL

If you catch a Pokémon with this ball, it will bond with you more easily when you start to train it.

6. DIVE BALL

This is a must-have for any Trainer who wants to capture rare Water Pokémon. If used underwater, your success of catching a Pokémon will increase more than threefold.

5. REPEAT BALL

Let's say you have a Pikachu, and you want another one. A Repeat Ball will let you catch a breed of Pokémon that you already have more easily.

4. GREAT BALL

This ball will give you an edge when trying to catch powerful Pokémon. It really improves your chances.

3. ULTRA BALL

Not as powerful as a Master Ball, an Ultra Ball is still good for catching high-level Pokémon.

2. MASTER BALL

If you want to catch rare Legendary Pokémon such as Mewtwo or Lugia, you'll have to have a Master Ball. This powerful ball can catch any Pokémon you toss it at (with just a few technical exceptions). It's simply the best.

1. POKÉ BALL

That's right. The regular, red-and-white Poké Ball gets the number one spot. Why? It might not be the most powerful ball, but it's definitely the most useful. They're cheap, easy to find, and can catch hundreds of different Pokémon. A true classic.

TOP 10 BATTLES

A good Pokémon battle will keep you on the edge of your seat, wondering what will happen next. The end might be more shocking than a Thundershock attack! Check out the battles that made our list.

10. PIKACHU VS. SPEAROW

What's key about this battle is what it meant to Ash and Pikachu. In the beginning, Pikachu didn't obey Ash at all. Then they were attacked by a flock of angry Spearow. Ash put himself in danger to save Pikachu, and Pikachu returned the favor by using the last of its power to defeat the Spearow. In that moment, they each knew they had a friend forever.

9. TYRANITAR & LARVITAR VS. THE POACHER BROTHERS

Never make a mother Tyranitar angry! That's a lesson the Pokémon Poacher Brothers learned the hard way. These thieves tried to capture a Tyranitar, keeping it away from its young Larvitar. Mistake! Tyranitar unleashed Hyper Beam after Hyper Beam to free itself and stop the poachers.

Larvitar fought by its mother's side, using Screech and Hidden Power. No wonder they call this the "Mother of All Battles!'"

8. TEAM ROCKET VS. BUTCH & CASSIDY

Jessie, James, and Meowth never seem to impress their boss the way Butch and Cassidy do. But when the two teams of Team Rocket goons fought over a captured Lugia, Jessie and James showed they could battle with the best. Jessie's Arbok and James's Weepinbell battled Cassidy's Houndour and Butch's Hitmontop. Jessie and James freed Lugia in the end. Sure, it was by accident — but a win is a win!

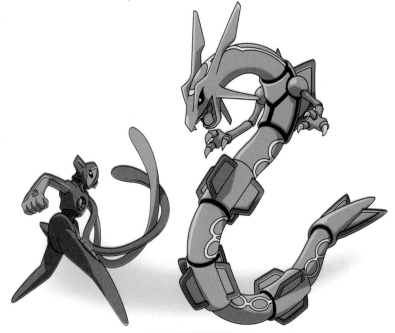

7. DEOXYS VS. RAYQUAZA

The battle began in the frozen north, when Deoxys fell from space, invading Rayquaza's territory. It ended in a busy city, where Rayquaza battled two Deoxys. It was a dazzling display of power moves against crippling Psychic attacks.

6. CHARIZARD VS. ARTICUNO

Ash won his first big victory in the Battle Frontier when he faced Noland — and his Legendary Pokémon Articuno! Charizard spit out Flamethrower. Articuno attacked with freezing Ice Beam. But in the end, Charizard won it all with a Seismic Toss.

5. ASH VS. GARY

This 6-on-6 battle at the Silver Conference showcased a variety of impressive Pokémon. Gary used Nidoqueen, Magmar, Scizor, Golem, Arcanine, and Blastoise. Ash used Tauros, Heracross, Muk, Bayleef, Snorlax, and Charizard. Both Trainers battled hard, but Pokémon fans everywhere cheered when Ash finally beat his rival.

4. ASH VS. MISTY

These two are longtime friends, but they have battled a few times. Misty lost once in a contest to see who would get to keep Totodile. But she bounced back when she faced Ash in the Whirl Cup Competition. In a surprise move, Misty's Psyduck came out of its Poké Ball accidentally and defeated Ash's Kingler!

3. CHARIZARD VS. ENTEI

This red-hot battle pitted Ash's Fire-type Pokémon against Entei, a Legendary Fire-type. Fireballs flew as these impressive Pokémon traded attack after attack. Charizard flew through the air, and Entei leaped and soared as though it had wings. Charizard fainted in the end, but luckily a little girl named Molly stopped Entei from doing further damage.

2. GROUDON VS. KYOGRE

These powerful Legendary Pokémon faced off when Team Magma and Team Aqua decided to mess with the forces of nature. Ages ago, it's said, these two giants had a battle that almost destroyed Earth. It almost happened again when the two took to the ocean in a huge fight. Hyper Beam and Solar Beam attacks flew, and Pikachu got possessed, but in the end, the world was safe once more.

1. MEW VS. MEWTWO

Pokémon fans still argue over which is the stronger Pokémon: Mew or its genetically engineered clone, Mewtwo. When Mewtwo created an army of Pokémon clones in hopes of taking over the world, Mew made a rare appearance and came to stop it. First, it tried to talk to Mewtwo. When that didn't work, the two engaged in a Psychic battle that almost tore apart the world of Pokémon. Ash risked his life to stop the battle, which ended in a draw. So the argument over which Pokémon is more powerful still rages on. . . .

ASH'S TOP 10 MOMENTS

We've rooted and cheered for Ash since the very beginning. We've shared in his triumphs and his disappointments. There are some moments we'll never forget. These are the 10 best ones ever!

10. I CAUGHT A CATERPIE!

It doesn't sound very thrilling. But for Ash Ketchum, a Pokémon Trainer just starting out on his journey, it was a major triumph. Caterpie was the first Pokémon Ash ever caught and started him down the road to becoming the incredible Pokémon Trainer he is today!

9. DESTROYING BICYCLES

Ash is usually pretty excited about his Pokémon. Sometimes, his excitement can get him into accidents. Early in his journey, he borrowed Misty's bike and then destroyed it. Later on, he did the same thing with May's bike. These two accidents were lucky for Ash because they brought him two great friends to share his journey with.

8. POKÉMON TEARS

When Mewtwo and Mew fought their historic battle, Ash was injured. As he lay motionless on the floor, all of the exhausted, no-longer-battling Pokémon gathered around. Touched that Ash would risk his life to save them, they began to cry. Their tears revived him!

7. THE WORLD WILL TURN TO ASH

An ancient prophecy of the Orange Islands talked about the Chosen One, someone who would save them from disaster. Ash never would have guessed that the prophecy was about him! Ash had to cross an icy island and battle three Legendary Pokémon, but he saved the day and fulfilled the prophecy.

6. THE BOULDER BADGE

Ash earned his very first badge when he battled Brock at the Pewter City Gym. Not only did he win, he also made a friend for life in Brock.

5. THE KNUCKLE BADGE

Ash's first battle with Brawly left his Treecko hurt and Ash feeling guilty. He vowed not to leave Dewford Town until he beat Brawly and earned his Knuckle Badge. After the rematch, Ash was triumphant and earned his badge.

4. THE ORANGE LEAGUE TROPHY

At Pummelo Island, Ash faced off against Drake, the Orange League Gym Leader. Ash beat Drake and his Dragonite and earned himself the Orange League Trophy. It also earned Ash and his Pokémon a place in the Hall of Heroes. Ash was the first person in the history of the Orange League to defeat Drake!

3. ASH BEATS GARY

Gary always made a big deal about being a better Trainer than Ash. He'd beaten Ash in battle, but the two took the field again in the first match of the Johto League Silver Conference. The battle of six on six Pokémon went back and forth until Gary was left with his Blastoise, and Ash had only his Charizard. It seemed like an uneven match — how could Charizard defend against powerful Water-type attacks? But Ash used strategy to finally defeat Gary.

2. PIKACHU CHOOSES ASH

At first, Ash wasn't sure if he would ever bond with his Pikachu. When they stumbled upon a group of wild Pikachu, Ash's Pikachu seemed so happy. Ash tearfully told his Pikachu to join its wild friends. But Pikachu chose to stay with Ash instead — and the rest is history!

1. SLEEPING LATE

It might have been unintentional, but sleeping late was one of the best things Ash ever did. The day Ash was to begin his Pokémon training, he overslept. If Ash had been on time, he would never have been given Pikachu. Gary Oak and two other Trainers made it to Professor Oak's lab first and took all the starter Pokémon. Pikachu was all the professor had left. We can't say how happy we are about Ash's mistake. Ash without Pikachu? Unthinkable!

If you are a Pokémon Trainer and want to win badges and make a name for yourself, you can't stay in Pallet Town. You've got to hit the road and find the toughest Gyms and the most exciting places to visit. Ash and his friends spend all of their time traveling from place to place. If you want to catch 'em all, you will have to travel far and wide, too. Here are the places you just can't miss.

10. SAFARI ZONE

You'll need a special pass to enter this area of the Kanto or Hoenn region, but it's worth it. There you can battle and capture a variety of wild Pokémon, including Aipom, Quagsire, and Octillery.

9. MT. SILVER

You've got to go here if you want to enter the Johto League Championship. Ash faced some his toughest opponents there, including his rival, Gary.

8. LAVARIDGE TOWN

Home to the Lavaridge Gym and the fiery Pokémon Trainer Flannery, this town is a must to visit if you want to pick up your Heat Badge. Need to relax before your battle? No problem in Lavaridge Town. Just head over to the town's hot springs and soak in the soothing waters. Ahhhhh.

7. BLACKTHORN CITY

If you love Dragon Pokémon, then Blackthorn City is the place for you! When Ash and friends first came to this city, the first thing they spotted was a Dratini sleeping along a riverbank. No wonder, because Blackthorn City Gym Leader Clair is a Dragon Pokémon specialist.

6. PALLET TOWN

Okay, we did say that you have to leave Pallet Town sometime. But it's worth going back once in a while to talk to Professor Oak. He's always got some new information to share!

5. POKÉMON CONTEST HALLS

Do you think your Slowking is the smartest Pokémon around? Or maybe your Feraligatr is the toughest? Maybe you think your Pichu is the cutest Pokemon ever. Then it's time to put your Pokémon to the test and head over to the nearest Contest Hall. If you need some advice, just ask May. She's entered and won many contests.

4. MT. CHIMNEY

Hot enough for you? If you need more excitement, then make your way to Mt. Chimney. There's always a lot of action going on at this fiery volcano. Trainers from all over the Pokémon world gather to battle here. It was also the scene of an epic battle between Team Magma and Team Aqua as they fought over a mysterious meteorite that had fallen to Earth.

3. THE ORANGE ISLANDS

If you like to explore and discover new things, then these tropical islands are for you. When Ash traveled there, he saw Pokémon he had never seen. He even stumbled on an island of Pokémon that had all turned the color pink!

2. THE WHIRL ISLANDS

Located in the Johto Region, these islands are home to a competitive tournament featuring Water-type Pokémon only. They're also one of the only places around where you can find the legendary Pokémon Lugia.

1. BATTLE FRONTIER

This is the ultimate playground for a Trainer who loves to battle. You can test your skill in a variety of different battle environments, including a Battle Dome and Battle Arena. You get to face expert Trainers. It's an amazing experience sure to raise your skill levels.

SECTION 4
TOP 10 BEST

Each Pokémon is special in its own way — every one has something to offer a Pokémon Trainer. That's why it's so difficult to pick the Top 10 Pokémon of All Time.

But we're going to do it anyway! This is our tribute to the Pokémon we just can't live without.

Like we said earlier, you're probably going to disagree with our choices. Don't worry! In this section, you get to choose your Top 10 Pokémon of All Time, too! You can pick your favorite Pokémon, the ones you've grown to love and depend on. It's your list, so you can do whatever you want.

So what are you waiting for? Let's count down the Top 10 Best of the best. . . .

TOP 10
POKÉMON OF ALL TIME

The Pokémon on this list are here because they're unique in a memorable way. Whether they're strong, loyal, or mysterious, they're all Pokémon that we are fascinated with. How do they stack up against *your* Top 10?

10. MEOWTH

That's right! It's not Legendary or powerful. But Meowth's cleverness and sense of humor are unforgettable. A world without Meowth would be way too boring.

9. LATIOS

This Legendary Pokémon can fly faster than a jet plane by folding its legs to minimize resistance. It's really intelligent, and can communicate with humans. In battle, it can make its opponent see images inside its head.

8. LATIAS

A companion to Latios, this Pokémon is unusually intelligent and sensitive to the emotions of others. Latias and Latios are both unusual for Legendary Pokémon because Latias is female and Latios is male.

7. CELEBI

This Pokémon has a sweet appearance that hides an amazing power. Celebi can travel through time.

6. MEWTWO

Its DNA is almost the same as Mew, and it has Psychic-type attacks, but Mewtwo and Mew are very different. Mewtwo was created in a lab for the sole purpose of winning battles. It lives in hiding, concentrating on raising its levels so that no one can beat it.

5. MEW

Researchers believe Mew is the ancestor of all Pokémon. This Pokémon is one of the most difficult to capture. If you do capture it, its super psychic powers will astonish you.

4. LUGIA

This Legendary Pokémon is a gentle giant. Its psychic powers are so strong that it has to live under the ocean, only rising when the world is in grave danger. Lugia is known as the Guardian of the Seas.

3. CHARIZARD

This powerhouse can breathe fire and fly. It's a combination that's hard to beat in battle. Ash's Charizard may have been difficult to train, but it's grown to become the one Pokémon that he counts on when he needs to save the day.

2. BLAZIKEN

Any Trainer who has evolved a Torchic into Combusken and then Blaziken will tell you why this Pokémon never leaves the lineup. Its Fire-and-Fighting-type combination means Blaziken packs a powerful punch. And unlike some hard-to-find Pokémon, every hardworking Trainer can raise a Blaziken.

1. PIKACHU

You can go around the world and ask Pokémon Trainers the name of their favorite Pokémon, and the answer is still, almost always, Pikachu! It's cute. Its Electric attacks deal out sizzling damage. It's extremely loyal. Pikachu is the total package, period.

YOUR OWN TOP 10

Here's your chance! Write your own list of Top 10 Greatest Pokémon. Go ahead and put Caterpie at number one — we can't stop you! This time, you call the shots.

10. _____ because _____

_____

9. _____ because _____

_____

8. _____ because _____

_____

7. _____ because _____

_____

6. _____

because _____

_____

5. _____

because _____

_____

4. _____

because _____

_____

_____

3. _____

because _____

_____

2. _____

because _____

_____

1. _____ because _____

_____

THE END? NO WAY!

Yes, Pokémon has been around for 10 years. We've seen hundreds of Pokémon and witnessed hundreds of battles. But things are just starting to get good.

In the world of Pokémon, the next adventure is always just around the corner. There are always new Pokémon to find, new places to explore, and new Trainers to battle.

We could make a list of Top 10 reasons to stick with Pokémon for another 10 years, but we won't. That's because you only need one reason:

Gotta catch 'em all!